marques vickers

DOWNTOWN SEATTLE
THE CONTEMPORARY SKYLINE

DOWNTOWN SEATTLE:
The Contemporary Skyline

MARQUIS PUBLISHING
HERRON ISLAND, WASHINGTON

TABLE OF CONTENTS

Holocaust Center for Humanity, 2045 Second Avenue

THIRD AVENUE
Pacific Building, 722 Third Avenue
Wells Fargo Center, 999 Third Avenue
Abraham Lincoln Building, 1110 Third Avenue
Expeditors International Building, 1015 Third Avenue
1111 Third Avenue Building
Washington Mutual Tower, 1201 Third Avenue
2031 Third Avenue Building, 2031 Third Avenue
Royal Crest Building, 2100 Third Avenue

FOURTH AVENUE
King County Administration Building, 500 Fourth Avenue
Seattle City Hall, 600 Fourth Avenue
Fourth and Madison Building, 925 Fourth Avenue
Seattle Public Library, 1000 Fourth Avenue
Safeco Plaza, 1001 Fourth Avenue
Hotel Monaco, 1101 Fourth Avenue
W Hotel, 1112 Fourth Avenue
Financial Center Building 1215 Fourth Avenue
Puget Sound Plaza, 1325 Fourth Avenue
Century Square Building, 1501 Fourth Avenue
1918-1922 Fourth Avenue Building
Fourth and Blanchard Building, 2101 Fourth Avenue
Arrive Building, 2116 Fourth Avenue

FIFTH AVENUE
300 Fifth Avenue Building
Chinook Building, 401 Fifth Avenue
Seattle Municipal Court Building, 600 Fifth Avenue
625 Fifth Avenue Building
Seattle Municipal Tower, 700 Fifth Avenue
Columbia Tower, 701 Fifth Avenue
Swedish Medical Center, 800 Fifth Avenue
The Mark Building, 801 Fifth Avenue

901 Fifth Avenue Building, 901 Fifth Avenue
Madison Centre, 920 Fifth Avenue
IBM Building, 1200 Fifth Avenue
Rainier Tower, 1301 Fifth Avenue
New Rainier Square Tower, 1301 Fifth Avenue
Motif Building, 1415 Fifth Street
US Bank Centre, 1420 Fifth Avenue
Westin Hotel, 1900 Fifth Avenue
2101 Fifth Avenue Building

SIXTH AVENUE
Crowne Plaza Hotel, 1113 Sixth Avenue
Park Place Building, 1200 Sixth Avenue
Hilton Hotel, 1301 Sixth Avenue
Sheraton Hotel, 1400 Sixth Avenue
Westin Building Exchange, 2001 Sixth Avenue
Jazz Alley, 2033 Sixth Avenue
2151 Sixth Avenue Building
Denny Building, 2200 Sixth Avenue

SEVENTH AVENUE
Qwest Plaza Building, 1600 Seventh Avenue
1700 Seventh Avenue Building
Amazon Doppler Building, 2021 Seventh Avenue
Amazon Spheres, 2101 Seventh Avenue
Amazon Day One Building, 2121 Seventh Avenue
Amazon Rufus Block 20 Building, 2100 Seventh Avenue
Amazon Rufus Block 18 Building, 2205 Seventh Avenue
Amazon Rufus Block 21 Building, 2220 Seventh Avenue
41-Story Apartment Building, 2301 Seventh Avenue

EIGHTH AVENUE
Hyatt at Olive 8, 1635 Eight Avenue
1918 Eighth Avenue Building
West Eight Building, 2001 Eighth Avenue
Cirrus Seattle, 2030 Eighth Avenue

Amazon re: Invent, 2121 Eighth Avenue
McKenzie Building, 2202 Eighth Avenue

NINTH AVENUE
Seattle Children's Research, 1900 Ninth Avenue
Stratus Building, 2101 Ninth Avenue
2200 Ninth Avenue Building

BATTERY STREET
Insigma Towers, 583 Battery Street

BLANCHARD STREET
820 Blanchard Street Building
Blanchard Plaza, 2201 Blanchard Street

BOREN AVENUE
1099 Boren Avenue North Building
Tilt49 Building, 1812 Boren Avenue
Hilton Gardens Hotel, 1821 Boren Avenue

DEXTER AVENUE N
Apple Computer Complex, 333 Dexter Avenue N

HOWELL STREET
Metropolitan Park North Building, 1220 Howell Street

JOHN STREET
820 John Street Building

LENORA STREET
Warwick Hotel, 401 Lenora Street

MADISON STREET
Ramada Renaissance Hotel, 515 Madison Street

MINOR AVENUE

Metropolitan Park East Building, 1730 Minor Avenue
NEXUS Seattle, 1808 Minor Avenue
Kinects Tower, 1823 Minor Avenue

OLIVE WAY
720 Olive Way Building
809 Olive Way Building
Metropolitan Park West Building, 1100 Olive Way

PIKE STREET
520 Pike Tower, 520 Pike Street

PINE STREET
Fifth Avenue Monorail Station, 400 Pine Street
Pacific Place Building, 600 Pine Street
Grand Hyatt Building, 721 Pine Street
Tower at 801, 801 Pine Street
Premier on Pine Building, 815 Pine Street

SOUTH KING STREET
201 King Street Center, 201 South King Street
Avalara Building, 255 South King Street Building
Wave Building, 521 South King Street

STEWART STREET
Plaza 600 Building, 600 Stewart Street
US District Federal Court, 700 Stewart Street
818 Stewart Street Building
1007 Stewart Street Building

TERRY AVENUE
103 Terry Avenue North Building
Amazon Kumo Building, 1915 Terry Avenue
Seattle Children's Hospital Building Cure, 1920 Terry
Avenue
Cornish Commons Building, 2025 Terry Avenue

Pan Pacific Hotel, 2125 Terry Avenue
2200 Terry Avenue Building
2201 Terry Avenue Building

UNION STREET
Four Seasons Hotel, 99 Union Street
Two Union Square, 601 Union Street

UNIVERSITY STREET
One Union Square, 600 University Street

WALL STREET
Spire Apartments, 600 Wall Street

WESTERN AVENUE
Post Building, 888 Western Avenue

WESTLAKE AVENUE
112 Westlake Avenue North Building
CitizenM Hotel, 201 Westlake Avenue North
Metropolitan Tower, 1492 Westlake Avenue

ABOUT THE AUTHOR

Version 1.3

Published by Marquis Publishing
Herron Island, Washington USA

Vickers, Marques, 1957

DOWNTOWN SEATTLE: The Contemporary Skyline
Vertical Washington Series

Dedicated to my Daughters Charline and Caroline.

Preface

Seattle is a hybrid urban center integrating historic with contemporary architecture. Vertical storied growth has been accentuated by the emergence of the high technology and bio-med business sectors and an absence of expandable space. Seattle's continued growth will be directly proportional to the expansion, innovation and evolution of these industries.

Historically the Seattle economy has been diversified with Boeing its most visible institution. Tech growth has accelerated the demands for office space, parking, residential housing and transportation solutions. Aggressive development has resulted in soaring rents, congestion and extreme gridlock.

The city of Seattle appears to be playing infrastructure catch-up. It has been justifiably observed that the city was never intended to expand into its present girth. Such observations become academic and antiquated when one views the fruition of its present vertical skyline. Even more developments remain in various stages of planning and completion. These structures have become the new permanence, a form of *neo-Urbania*. Retreat and constraint are no longer options or alternatives.

This is not the first occasion when Seattle has undergone a complete transformation. The great fire of June 6, 1889 obliterated the entire central business district. The inferno destroyed 25 city blocks and forever altered the nature and composition of future construction projects.

Wooden buildings were banned in the burned out sectors to be replaced by brick and stone. The street levels were likewise elevated in some areas up to twenty-two feet. Nostalgia for the past layout was noticeably absent amidst the haste to rebuild and reestablish commercial continuity. The old city became simply a layer of subterranean strata.

Many of these post-fire masonry structures remain intact today and integrate seamlessly into the fabric of Seattle's downtown. This same integration may not be observed within some of the older residential districts. Queen Anne, Ballard and Capital Hill remain reminders of simpler transportation requirements and cloistered spacing. Their narrow streets and avenues demand precarious maneuvering and often single sided street parking. Many defy the space requirements for dual direction driving and vehicle dents become as common as the sustaining winter rains.

This quaint intimacy and inefficiency remains archaically impractical with the surrounding improvements and development. Solutions for correction remain few and most are not viable due to space constraints.

Future visions for a vibrant downtown core stream forward. Obstacles will be addressed and the faint cries of protest will likely be overruled. With each subsequent constructed monolith, Seattle solidifies its claim towards twenty-first century credibility and stature.

Growth becomes an insatiable surge. For the high technology industry to maintain its frenetic pace, progress is essential. Perhaps one day, Seattle and such a volatile industry will arrive at a crossroad where sustaining such expansion becomes problematic and unsustainable. For now, there remains the identical absence of hesitation as the city experienced over a century before after its near cataclysmic annihilation.

The images in this edition were initially photographed during the autumn of 2016 and have continued through 2021. The intent of this series is to document an evolving Seattle skyline as major components are completed and fill in the pieces, much like a jigsaw puzzle. The process is far from complete and future editions will reflect the continued growth.

FIRST AVENUE

Loews Hotel
1000 First Avenue

Watermark Tower,
1107 First Avenue

2+U Tower
1201 Second Avenue

2+U Tower, 1201 Second Avenue

Seattle Art Museum, 1300 First Avenue

Seattle Art Museum, 1300 First Avenue

Harborsteps Northeast Tower, 1305 First Avenue

Harborsteps Northeast Tower, 1305 First Avenue

First Union Building
1401 First Avenue

1609 First Avenue Building

Sequel Apartments, 1900 First Avenue

2016

One Pacific Tower, 2000 First Avenue

One Pacific Tower, 2000 First Avenue

Market Place Tower, 2025 First Avenue

Market Place Tower, 2025 First Avenue

2127 First Avenue Building

2127 First Avenue Building

Bell Tower, 2127 First Avenue

Volta Luxury Apartments, 2233 First Avenue

Volta Luxury Apartments, 2233 First Avenue

2323 First Avenue Building

2323 First Avenue Building

SECOND AVENUE

Millennium Tower, 719 Second Avenue

Henry M. Jackson Federal Building 915 Second Avenue

Henry M. Jackson Federal Building, 915 Second Avenue

Seattle Trust Tower, 1000 Second Avenue

Seattle Trust Tower, 1000 Second Avenue

Safeco Center, 1191 Second Avenue

Newmark Tower, 1401 Second Avenue

West Edge Building, 1430 Second Avenue

Fifteen Twenty-One Building, 1521 Second Avenue

Fifteen Twenty One Building, 1521 Second Avenue

2O16

Helios Building, 1600 Second Avenue

Helios Building, 1600 Second Avenue

Charter Hotel, 1610 Second Avenue

Charter Hotel, 1610 Second Avenue

The Emerald Condominiums, 1613 Second Avenue

The Emerald Condominiums, 1613 Second Avenue

Viktoria Apartments, 1915 Second Avenue

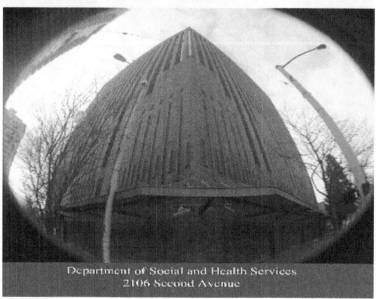

Department of Social and Health Services
2106 Second Avenue

Tower 12 Apartments, 2015 Second Avenue

2020 Second Avenue Building

Holocaust Center for Humanities
2045 Second Avenue

THIRD AVENUE

Pacific Building, 722 Third Avenue

Wells Fargo Center, 999 Third Avenue

Wells Fargo Center, 999 Third Avenue

Abraham Lincoln Building, 1110 Third Avenue

Expeditors International Building, 1015 Third Avenue

1111 Third Avenue Building

Washington Mutual Tower, 1201 Third Avenue

Washington Mutual Tower, 1201 Third Avenue

Washington Mutual Tower, 1201 Third Avenue

2031 Third Avenue Building, 2031 Third Avenue

2031 Third Avenue Building

Royal Crest, 2100 Third Avenue

FOURTH AVENUE

King County Administration Building, 500 Fourth Avenue

Seattle City Hall, 600 Fourth Avenue

Seattle City Hall, 600 Fourth Avenue

Seattle City Hall, 600 Fourth Avenue

Fourth and Madison Building, 925 Fourth Avenue

Fourth and Madison Building, 925 Fourth Avenue

Seattle Public Library, 1000 Fourth Avenue

Seattle Public Library, 1000 Fourth Avenue

Seattle Public Library, 1000 Fourth Avenue

Seattle Public Library, 1000 Fourth Avenue

Safeco Plaza, 1001 Fourth Avenue

Safeco Plaza, 1001 Fourth Avenue

Hotel Monaco, 1101 Fourth Avenue

W Hotel, 1112 Fourth Avenue

Financial Center Building 1215 Fourth Avenue

Puget Sound Plaza, 1325 Fourth Avenue

Century Square Building, 1501 Fourth Avenue

Century Square Building, 1501 Fourth Avenue

1918-1922 Fourth Avenue Building

1918-1922 Fourth Avenue Building

Fourth and Blanchard Building, 2101 Fourth Avenue

Fourth and Blanchard Building, 2101 Fourth Avenue

Arrive B uilding, 2116 Fourth Avenue

FIFTH AVENUE

300 Fifth Avenue Building

300 Fifth Avenue Building

Chinook Building, 401 Fifth Avenue

Chinook Building, 401 Fifth Avenue

Seattle Municipal Court Building, 600 Fifth Avenue

625 Fifth Avenue Building

Seattle Municipal Tower, 700 Fifth Avenue

Seattle Municipal Tower, 700 Fifth Avenue

Seattle Municipal Tower, 700 Fifth Avenue

Columbia Tower, 701 Fifth Avenue

Columbia Tower, 701 Fifth Avenue

Columbia Tower, 701 Fifth Avenue

Columbia Tower, 701 Fifth Avenue

Swedish Medical Center, 800 Fifth Avenue

Swedish Medical Center, 800 Fifth Avenue

2016

The Mark Building, 801 Fifth Avenue

2016

The Mark Building, 801 Fifth Avenue

The Mark Building, 801 Fifth Avenue

The Mark Building, 801 Fifth Avenue

901 Fifth Avenue Building, 901 Fifth Avenue

901 Fifth Avenue Building, 901 Fifth Avenue

Madison Centre, 920 Fifth Avenue

IBM Building, 1200 Fifth Avenue

IBM Building, 1200 Fifth Avenue

IBM Building, 1200 Fifth Avenue

2016

Rainier Square, 1301 Fifth Avenue

2016

Rainier Square, 1301 Fifth Avenue

Rainier Square, 1301 Fifth Avenue

New Rainier Square Tower, 1301 Fifth Avenue

Rainier Square, 1301 Fifth Avenue

Rainier Square, 1301 Fifth Avenue

Rainier Square, 1301 Fifth Avenue

Motif Building, 1415 Fifth Street

US Bank Centre, 1420 Fifth Avenue

US Bank Centre, 1420 Fifth Avenue

Westin Hotel, 1900 Fifth Avenue

Westin Hotel, 1900 Fifth Avenue

2101 Fifth Avenue Building

2101 Fifth Avenue Building

SIXTH AVENUE

Crowne Plaza Hotel, 1113 Sixth Avenue

Crowne Plaza Hotel, 1113 Sixth Avenue

Park Place Building, 1200 Sixth Avenue

Hilton Hotel, 1301 Sixth Avenue

Sheraton Hotel, 1400 Sixth Avenue

Westin Building Exchange, 2001 Sixth Avenue

Jazz Alley, 2033 Sixth Avenue

2131 Sixth Avenue Building

Denny Building, 2200 Sixth Avenue

SEVENTH AVENUE

Qwest Plaza Building, 1600 Seventh Avenue

1700 Seventh Avenue Building

Amazon Doppler Building, 2021 Seventh Avenue

Amazon Doppler Building, 2021 Seventh Avenue

Amazon Doppler Building, 2021 Seventh Avenue

Amazon Doppler Building, 2021 Seventh Avenue

Amazon Spheres, 2101 Seventh Avenue

Amazon Spheres, 2101 Seventh Avenue

2016

Amazon Day One Building, 2121 Seventh Avenue

2016

Amazon Day One Building, 2121 Seventh Avenue

2016

Amazon Day One Building, 2121 Seventh Avenue

Amazon Day One Building, 2121 Seventh Avenue

Amazon Rufus Block 20 Building, 2100 Seventh Avenue

Amazon Rufus Block 20 Building, 2100 Seventh Avenue

Amazon Rufus Block 18 Building. 2205 Seventh Avenue

Amazon Rufus Block 18 Building. 2205 Seventh Avenue

Amazon Rufus Block 18 Building, 2205 Seventh Avenue

Amazon Rufus Block 18 Building, 2205 Seventh Avenue

2019

Amazon Rufus Block 21 Building, 2220 Seventh Avenue

Amazon Rufus Block 21 Building, 2220 Seventh Avenue

Amazon Rufus Block 21 Building, 2220 Seventh Avenue

41-Story Apartment Building, 2301 Seventh Avenue

41-Story Apartment Building, 2301 Seventh Avenue

EIGHTH AVENUE

Hyatt at Olive 8, 1635 Eighth Avenue

1918 Eighth Avenue Building

West Eighth Building, 2001 Eighth Avenue

Cirrus Seattle, 2030 Eighth Avenue

Amazon re:Invent Building, 2121 Eighth Avenue

Amazon re:Invent Building, 2121 Eighth Avenue

McKenzie Building, 2202 Eighth Avenue

NINTH AVENUE

Seattle Children's Research, 1900 Ninth Avenue

2016

Stratus Building, 2101 Ninth Avenue

Stratus Building, 2101 Ninth Avenue

2200 Ninth Avenue Building

BATTERY STREET

Insigma Towers, 583 Battery Street

Insigma Towers, 583 Battery Street

BLANCHARD STREET

Amazon Regrade, 720 Blanchard Street

Amazon Regrade, 720 Blanchard Street

820 Blanchard Street Building

Blanchard Plaza, 2201 Blanchard Street

BOREN AVENUE

1099 Boren Avenue North Building

2016

Tilt49 Building, 1812 Boren Avenue

Tilt49 Building, 1812 Boren Avenue

Hilton Gardens Hotel, 1821 Boren Avenue

DEXTER AVENUE N

Apple Computer Complex, 333 Dexter Avenue N

Apple Computer Complex, 333 Dexter Avenue N

HOWELL STREET

Metropolitan Park North Building, 1220 Howell Street

JOHN STREET

820 John Street Building

LENORA STREET

Warwick Hotel, 401 Lenora Street

MADISON STREET

Ramada Renaissance Hotel, 515 Madison Street

MINOR AVENUE

Metropolitan Park East Building, 1730 Minor Avenue

NEXUS Seattle, 1808 Minor Avenue

NEXUS Seattle, 1808 Minor Avenue

2016

Kinects Tower, 1823 Minor Avenue (2016)

Kinects Tower, 1823 Minor Avenue

OLIVE WAY

720 Olive Way Building

809 Olive Way Building

Metropolitan Park West Building, 1100 Olive Way

PIKE STREET

520 Pike Tower, 520 Pike Street

PINE STREET

Fifth Avenue Monorail Station, 400 Pine Street

Pacific Place Building, 600 Pine Street

Grand Hyatt Building, 721 Pine Street

Tower at 801, 801 Pine Street

Premier on Pine Building, 813 Pine Street

SOUTH KING STREET

201 King Street Center, 201 South King Street

201 King Street Center, 201 South King Street

201 King Street Center, 201 South King Street

2016

Avalara Building, 255 South King Street

Avalara Building, 255 South King Street Building

The Wave Building, 521 South King Street

The Wave Building, 521 South King Street

STEWART STREET

Plaza Building, 600 Stewart Street

US District Federal Court, 700 Stewart Street

US District Federal Court, 700 Stewart Street

818 Stewart Street Building

1007 Stewart Street Building

TERRY AVENUE

103 Terry Avenue North Building

Amazon Kumo Building, 1915 Terry Avenue

Amazon Kumo Building, 1915 Terry Avenue

2019

Seattle Children's Hospital Building Cure, 1920 Terry Avenue

Seattle Children's Hospital Building Cure
1920 Terry Avenue

Seattle Children's Hospital Building Cure
1920 Terry Avenue

Cornish Commons Building, 2025 Terry Avenue

Pan Pacific Hotel, 2125 Terry Avenue

2200 Terry Avenue Building

2201 Terry Avenue Building

UNION STREET

Four Seasons Hotel, 99 Union Street

Two Union Square, 601 Union Street

UNIVERSITY STREET

One Union Square, 600 University Street

One Union Square, 600 University Street

WALL STREET

Spire Apartments, 600 Wall Street

Spire Apartments, 600 Wall Street

WESTERN AVENUE

Post Building, 888 Western Avenue

WEST LAKE AVENUE

112 Westlake Avenue North Building

CitizenM Hotel, 201 Westlake Avenue N

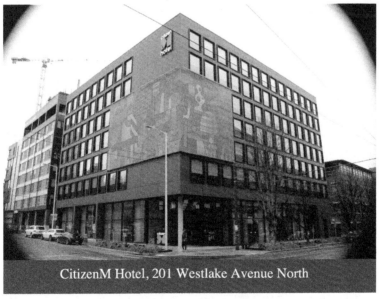

CitizenM Hotel, 201 Westlake Avenue North

Metropolitan Tower, 1492 Westlake Avenue

Author and Photographer Marques Vickers was born in 1957 in Vallejo, California. He graduated from Azusa Pacific University in Los Angeles and became the Director of the Burbank Chamber of Commerce between 1979-84.

Professionally, he has operated travel, apparel, and publishing businesses. His paintings and sculptures have been exhibited in art galleries and museums in the United States and Europe. He has previously lived in the Burgundy and Languedoc regions of France and currently lives on Herron Island in western Washington.

He has written and published over seventy books on a variety of subjects including the art and auction industry, architecture, wine, travel, crime, social satire and fiction.

Made in the USA
Las Vegas, NV
06 June 2023

73053480R00125